by Hayden Carruth

The Crow and the Heart
(Poems, 1959)

Journey to a Known Place
(A Long Poem, 1961)

The Norfolk Poems
(1962)

Appendix A
(A Novel, 1963)

North Winter
(Poems, 1964)

After the Stranger
Imaginary Dialogues with Camus (1965)

Nothing for Tigers
(Poems, 1965)

Notl

Nothing
for Tigers

Poems 1959–1964

by Hayden Carruth

The Macmillan Company, New York

Collier-Macmillan Limited, London

First printing

The Macmillan Company, New York
Collier-Macmillan Canada Ltd., Toronto, Ontario

Library of Congress catalog number: 65-12853

DESIGNED BY RONALD FARBER

Printed in the United States of America

Acknowledgments

Some of the poems in this book first appeared in the following publications: *The Carleton Miscellany, Chelsea, Chicago Choice, Chicago Daily News, The Hudson Review, The Kenyon Review, The Nation, New Republic, Poetry Northwest, Saturday Review,* and *The Virginia Quarterly Review.* "The Saving Way," "The Cheat," "Midsummer Letter," "Stanzas from the Reading Hour," "Spring Notes from Robin Hill," and "The Smallish Son" were first published in *Poetry.* "Sometimes My Huge Death Rips" and "The Master, Grieved with Age" were first published in *The New York Times.* "Essay on Marriage" was first published in *The Massachusetts Review.* "Light in the Locust Tree" was originally published as "In the Norfolk Hills" in *Audience,* copyright © Audience 1963; "The Profit of Gallant Verse" and "Christmas Present" were originally published in *Audience,* copyright © Audience 1963; "Thalassa" was originally published in *New Mexico Quarterly,* copyright © The University of New Mexico Press 1960; "Now" was originally published as "A Week After" in *Yankee,* copyright © Yankee, Inc. 1962.

Dedicated to old friends,

including

Jim Cunningham and Henry Rago

contents

part three

*The epigraphs at the beginning of each section
are the author's free adaptations.*

part one

The boy
With bittersweet in his hair lifted his hand
Modestly, and by the dark scuppers came lynxes.
Tigers and panthers came, beasts of shadow, hard
To be seen yet terrible, and the sailors leapt
To the sea, from fear or possibly from madness.
First to dive, first to shimmer in sea-change,
Whiteness trembling into the blur of dolphin,
Was Medon.
                                        —*Metamorphoses*

Song for Sara

Yes, I know, I did go in unto the Egyptian bondwoman,
Hagar in her dark tent,
Wherefore the child Ishmael is like to an evil foeman

Against me now, my own soul unvanquished and unspent.
Also I know
How you became again my sister in wonderment

And gave your pride willingly in the house of Pharaoh
And to Abimelech
The Philistine, because I feared your beauty. God bestow

Comfort upon you. Yet remember, it was we set this tent stake
In these warm hills
Of Canaan, we two together, two blessed by Melchizedek,

The truthful priest. Alone, neither of us fulfills
Or even understands
The terms time drives like tent stakes in our wills.

Perhaps for this I gave into your hands
The Egyptian maid,
And for this great kings unswore their demands

Upon you, returning you, so that I who had been afraid
Bore the shame then.
Now you laugh. In your bitterness for love delayed

You ask if the nerves shall sparkle at my touch again.
Sara, your laughter
Is a little solemn fox, the denizen

Of my heart's cave barking in his sleep, yet softer,
Sister, than Hebron's bees
Among the lilies. Your voice sorrows me. After

The journeys, the alien faces, the languages all p's
And q's, the wars,
A nephew in hot water, and now riches, this goodness and ease,

After God's voice like phosphor in the firs
At Bethel, the angels
Conversing with me in the twilight out of doors

And on the hills, after all this still memory jangles
Like a bell gone false,
Clacking self-ignorance, self-fear, the lie that mingles

In everything we think. The heart beats, the will halts.
Princess, my sister and wife,
Forgive me, it is I who fail. And God, who exalts,

Comes to our tent now, bidding us to life
After all,
Bidding us give what we are, scabbard and knife.

What we are. Love means to use, to make use of, to recall
Every taste of the years,
Choosing this, the best that we are, two even in downfall,

O wife, sister, princess, mother of hope. Tears,
Fears,
No, they are gone. This homely song alone must sing in your ears.

Fantasie for St. Cecilia's Day

Perhaps zephyr of May just beginning
From nowhere, tinkling birch leaves
And sun's perspicuous cantabile disciplining
The water's early rapture, reprieves
Of sparklement, bestowals that glisten
Below a Japanese bridge
Where the stepsister swans so gravely listen,
Collegians of the occult purity. And the personage
Moving among birches
Without love, swaying her long blonde hair,
There is conducting her researches
Into the motiveless ecstasy her mind may soon declare.

Or again brown breeze of November
Ominously unspirited, sad trilling
Of desperate separate leaf-voices, an ember
Of sun, mauve sun, chilling
The black pool in obsessive pink, under
The curving emergencies of swans-in-flight,
A thunder
Oblique to the bridge. Flimsy and white,
The woman of the ashen tresses
Arches to her anguish without hate
In which cold souls of votaresses
Unfold in power and fiercely meditate.

Without love, without hate, she muses in symbolic stone,
The timeless upon time charming a thought
In blind passion, prior to the phrases of the moon,
And blind, too blind to see out!
Swansong, swansong, thought's angel calls the tune,
Turn and turn about.

The Swamp of Love

Redwing, alighting, rocks on his spar of reed,
"Ocheree" jocosely, "ocheree" with merriment.
Sunlight of March wimples the swamp,
Frayed and pale as worn wool, warming
The skunk cabbage barely and one astonished frog.

> Sing me, sweet, the blowing rose,
> North is a land of departing snows.

The swampside bank inclines, shall one say, softly?
Its boulders, loaves among the grass,
Afford an impression of waiting
As if for an honest couple,
As if for Pyrrha and Deucalion
Dumpish and potbellied from some Thessalian farm.
"Ocheree" sharply, "ocheree" with loudness,
"Ocheree," if the truth were told, a trifle coarsely.
And the south is a thing that comes from a very far sky;
Indeed, the south is a wrinkled ancient calligrapher,
Say from Hai-nan, with eyes like dirty pennies,
Brushing his delicate ribald letters exiguously
On the back of your hand.

> Sing me, sweet, the blowing rose,
> The frightening distance a poor thought goes.

In a garden of the great iris flowering
Like hearts of unicorns all plucked out for view,
Beneath the tree that is called pecan,
A woman in the thirty-sixth year of her life sits reading,
Reading (she writes) the dramas of Strindberg,
Smoking a cigarette, and with one foot
Jigging above the ground;

And her body
Contains wisdom and beauty like a book
With a bright cover and butterfly pages
Slowly rising and falling in soft revelations;
And is also in some respects like to a spice closet,
Being nutmeg-brown and in some parts obscure
But in others light, and being
Of the good odor of citron
Or, it may be, of mace
Or of another
Known to those who have acquaintance of fine things.

    Sing me, sweet, the blowing rose,
    Poetry talking as if it were prose.

Dear chosen history, so dear alien tongue,
My English tuning the scene baroque, the style
Of frolic waged among huge formal beds
All to the end of cavalier cast low,
Is he the tyrant still, that aureate boy
Whose barbs you rue in numbers sweetly pure?
Is that affection cruel, that bond still hard,
Ruling us, masters, greatly in your lines
For ears time-schooled and fondly orthodox?
"Ocheree" barbarously, "ocheree" like a hooting jade.
And the woman rises, putting away her book,
Yawning perhaps in unformed annoyance,
And looks upward through young leaves of pecan,
Up to the north sky,
Remarking the absence of clouds.
Is not a tedium to be found in the
Dramas of Strindberg? Reading
Is an act of patience—waiting, waiting—
And patience is perhaps less an act
Than one's arteries like the bruise-flowered wisteria
Seeking to root in the ground.

Sing me, sweet, the blowing rose,
Annual yesses, annual noes.

Hear the swamp now. The reeds are
Swaying and
Clacking. Already southern voices begin,
Talking severally and satisfactorily.
Then this is the manner of assurance—
Not fear, as in intimidation,
Not hopelessness, not servility,
Not, though pain stays, constrainment.
"Ocheree" triumphantly, "ocheree" with realism.
Liberator! In sorrowing distance,
Severing luck,
Loss,
Still this creating call to the new world comes,
Poems and more, the mind's days well encountered,
O Bolivar, intelligent and free!

The Diver

> "... *that monstrous thing,*
> *Returned and yet unrequited love.*"
> —*Yeats*

In dreams one does not work for pay.
The light is successful, layering
Light, rumpled sheets spreading
Undulantly, a white bed of vapors.
I am pretending that I am dreaming.

Above, distantly, a curlew cries.
Is it that odors of the sea
Are suggested by the curlew crying?
The sky flaps, cloth of heraldry,
A curlew crucified on the moon.

Clutch and claw the oily light.
Dreaming is such vague pretense.
Downward, clearly and covertly
The precious thing is disclosing itself,
The whiteness and loveliness waiting.

I descend. Claw and stroke.
Smooth troughs of the briny light.
Rescue, retrieve. Light seethes
In orchestral dilations, violins
Broken by the curlew crying,

And now I am remembering, the curlew
Is at best a myth, the invention
Of foreign poets. Alas! But you are
White, precious thing, white arms
And legs poised in the dark silts.

Stroke. Crawl. Take. Embrace.
The beady light combs my shoulders,
Frothing on wings that reach, hold,
Sweep back ample shocks of light,
Drinking great drafts of downwardness.

You call in the gloom, precious thing,
Ancient thing. You are tilting
Open-eyed in the green darkness.
You are giving me closer and closer
Anticipations, unmoving thing,

Discoveries in the rare extremes
Of light where you lie broken, O
Exquisite of the forsaken primitives!
I am reaching, unfurled like a long
Serpent searching the light's wake,

And the soft light of my fingertips
Is streaming, reaching, glowing on you.
But I am dreaming a doom-sudden pain,
Gloom-suffering and implosion of light
In tatters and fainting cacophonies!

There is slow tumbling now. I twist
In a crawling arc, sprawl, fall
Upward, a puff of scattering flakes.
I am dreaming that I am awake.
I lie shattered in a wrack of light,

Shreds drifting in a salt wind's sighing
And the curlew crying on the moon.
Brightly, covertly, the white thing
Shimmers unmoved in the green darkness.
I am pretending to remember my dream.

Midsummer Letter

Dearest: Today was warm.
  I sprayed the roses,
Pumping on our old-fashioned
Sprayer as if psychosis
Itself had taught my arm
  To be impassioned,

And thinking on you gone.
  You know that white
Mold that attacks the leaf
Like mildew, that damned blight
That crusts the bud? That one,
  Rosegrower's grief?

I think I may have thought
    If I had fury
And just sprayed hard enough
Somehow I'd get that sorry
And dank infection out
    Of me and off

Our roses too. I tried.
    We'll see what happens.
We've grown patient of riddles
Now our third movement opens,
The scherzo years, and pride
    Falls to the fiddles,

Prancing like those gay-suited
    Beggars at Rome's
Destruction. See, tomorrow
Like some great mania comes,
Instantly though deep-rooted
    In distant sorrow.

Granted, that root's the thorn
    Really. Our ages
Recall for us those summers
Spent too in spraying. Rage is
Incessantly forlorn:
    Mold or newcomers

Always resumed, the thrips,
    The worm or beetle.
I'll tell you what I think.
(These days my mind's a nettle
I can't let loose. It nips
    Me. Do you blink?)

I think of health. How willing
    Two wounded people
Can be to beg its chrism

Under some stainless steeple!
Yet isn't this the killing
    Absolutism?

The old pope in us? Well,
    I think you take
My meaning. You do see
(For love's sake, for *life's* sake)
Perfection's drive to quell
    Our need to be?

"To be." See how it was
    Before we came;
Our kind, I mean. The mold
Was suffered, so. No shame,
No censure; and the rose
    Kept its foothold

And bloomed. Lion his tick
    And tick his germ,
Eater and eaten, blight
And blighted, all confirm
Me. (Yes, my rhetoric
    Too, the birthright!)

Because just being eaten
    Was secondary
Always. Existence counts,
Petals that wax and carry
The painful mold hardbitten,
    Deep sap that mounts.

Then will the wild rose be
    A prettier joy?
Dear, not than our rose garden—
Occasionally. But say,
Shall beauty come to me
    As ward or warden?

Besides, the plant in nature—
   Soiled, torn—attracted
Our artist, bee, whose duty
Made meaning there, exacted
From use an acting pleasure,
   Definable beauty.

My point comes clearer. Our
   Domestic plant
Tends to pure form, abstract.
God knows, you've heard me rant
Often enough: the power
   Is form intact

In substance, etc., form
   As work, the thing
In action, not merely
A shape unfilled, a wing
Stilled in the—
                    Blast! I charm
   Myself (obscurely)

With terms licked from my betters,
   Philosophizing.
A curse, I grant you. More,
It creeps in here like poison,
Fouling these lovelorn matters
   With this uproar

Of thinking. Yet—the mold,
   Ascending, creeping,
Scaling me. And you, you!
Don't you burn when you're sleeping?
And tell me, is the child—
   This minute, now—

Burning? I fear it, know it,
     Sense it in your
Remoteness. How my nostril
Quivers against her fire!
In this way must we grow? It
     Seems the ancestral

Gist in the living moment
     Remakes us old
And maybe wise. A thought
I cannot help but hold
Upon our truth of torment
     As absolute

Is imperfectibility.
     Such is my case
Then. Having not one ounce
Or inch of churchly grace,
I say that dignity
     Is what remains

From all we thought we had
     To make defense
Against the creeping scale.
Dignity. What it means
Is—well, being afraid,
     Of course, but while

One lives to take in earnest
     The body's wish
For joy in the world's turning
Without one ounce or inch—
Look! Do you see, my dearest?
     The bush is burning . . .

So much while spraying. Sun
   Hung on the noon
Like damask, and the air
Clung hot to ending June,
The still solstice. My own
   Shone everywhere,

Roses, roses—fanged stems,
   The thorny snarl,
A tendril swaying down
To rip you, clutch, unfurl
The knots of bright bloodflames
   Leaping (a crown!)

Across the brow; and blooms,
   Yes, all those flowers,
Red too or a dying color,
Dripping their fragile powers
In petals and perfumes
   To quench my dolor.

Creatures of my despair,
   These lacerations
Blooming upon the season
Teach me, my dear, some patience
And somewhat more of care
   And much of reason.

A joy—homely, intense—
   I think will give
Us grace of our dispersal
Into the relative,
For only there we sense
   The universal.

Nor, finally, do I blather
　　Of mass alone,
The species that survives.
I speak the imperfect one
And one still caught together,
　　And their true lives.

Comforts of Granite

Comforts of granite, lichened and silvery as plush
Warming a paisley hill, or else the corn
In juba raised, soprano seven o'clock
Of an August morning, drenched in dew, or else—
When I am old I'll say these were a world.
See how the light in my remembrance hums
With gnatlike tensions where the willows burn
Bronzen in noon. And more, more. The lost boy
Whose felt simplicities create the land,
This land, kneels in his dark corner, takes
A quaint brown volume from the shelf of home,
Meaningless now, the dear and envied Greek.
I think I articled my works and days
For honest poems built to an honest land,
But some plowed beach and some the asphalt yard,
And who grew least it's difficult to say.
Measure us now, old earth. Renunciations
Bloom in the wisdom of a failed desire,
Autumnal failure rising forever now.
Something there is Novembers us and lays
The shriveling memories blackly at our feet.
Seconds puke with change. The highway's cord,
The suburb's fishnet spread—entelechies
Extending, searching, strangling, burying.

The land was like an intuition of history,
Mysterious as a navel, seldom seen,
Like ballast fuel in the mind's deep bunkers.
Grown up half way or less, I knew the change,
My sister crying somewhere in the sky,
But then forgot—experience possesses
Its innate anesthesia. So I have heard
Others remark before me, other survivors,
Enemies and friends. Fa la, fa la,
Henceforth I shall recite in gaudy tones
My chansons to the god of cities, fa la!
Though I can hear my old black mongrel Jock
Barking somewhere on the other side of the woods.

How to Write a Poem

The man he was made sullen and skinned prey
To sorrow's vulture stooping on his bone
In cassock wings, the year grown beaked and tall,
Poking the four bleached decades for a way
That love's poor fool, locked up, could have a son;
And loss and loss rang bell-like in his skull.
Loss, loss like a senior and baleful gong
Throbbing his expectations deeply stopped—
Lunacy's spongy, adventitious blow,
His eight-year solitude, a dreaming tongue
Wried on the alum name of a boy still trapped
And running in his loins forever now.
The artist he was, thinking how to warm
Some rhymes on his emotion, tried to speak
Contritely to the fathers, after Yeats,
Tried to apologize (with nice alarm)
And tell the sires how Yeatsian an ache
He bore to know he'd bring the line to quits;

Tried, if the truth were told, two times and then,
Seeing the poems like chickenbones on the page,
Rose up in loathing and destroyed them both,
Because the scheme could not keep feeling in,
That splendid scheme made in another age,
In another land, and God knows in another faith.
The United States: a rather astringent name
For astringent virtues. Well, the sires were lost,
Scattered from "Narragansett No. 6"
Into the West they thought they overcame,
Leaving him, born to the city, no bequest
Except the formal agony of his sex.
So much. Now, in a ruined year, he thought he saw
Something retrievable, a broken love
That might make wholeness still if it could force
The mind to image-seeking. Could he know
Continuance in the poem, be conscious of
A sexed mind driving some defining course
On voids of love? Uncharted ancestral reefs
Sank the poem, its only sail, the self,
Writhed on the green, quick-scattering foam.
He cried out, "Christ!" He held out all his griefs
Like offerings to a grave angelic dwarf
To steal away his being and take it home.
But cowards make fools. Sick men know best. He knew
The good self as corrosive lineament,
Being as a symbol's content wrecked
In the symbol's desuetude. The personal view
Is all, a rent man patched till the final rent
And comic end. Hope is the thief of fact.
The family was a dream, the boy a myth
Imagined as the continuance of his pride
In being, the fiction given in a name;
Desire to be was the substitute for faith.
He, the American, knowing he could not hide
The difficult or the ugly in his time,
Made of the boy a thought to put away

Like other vanity of brains or looks.
In bravery or in wisdom—who can say?—
He nursed his broken love and wrote his books.

Parable

Snow falls; I furnish seed to winter birds;
A squirrel eats it, deaf to my hard words.

In barren pine flit junco and blue jay;
The squirrel occupies the feeding tray.

Eating, he takes an attitude of prayer,
Appeasing *his* god, clearly, with *my* fare.

He feasts to save his soul? O wicked food
That fills his stomach in ingratitude!

For he grows fat and jays grow lean, and dusk
Leaves me for my content a tray of husk.

Words for Thin Voice and Gently Twanging Mandolin

You almost got me, baby doll,
    Yes, you almost got me,
When you took my gun, my pretty little gun,
    And aimed it and shot me.

That silvery bullet, baby doll,
  Yes, that silvery bullet,
It hung me limp in the throbbing air
  Like some plucked pullet.

Who said don't worry, baby doll,
  Yes, who said don't worry?
Was it you in my glistening, sterile room,
  Weeping and sorry?

Maybe you came there, baby doll,
  Yes, maybe you came there,
And maybe you brought me the drooping rose
  For my wound's shame there.

When I recover, baby doll,
  Yes, when I recover,
I'll touch your hair and kiss your eyes,
  And you will do it all over.

The Profit of Gallant Verse

The profit of gallant verse
That in fancy posed my dear
With Helen of old times
Was a mistress who could jeer,
If gently, and put a curse,
If lightly, on all love-rhymes.
"Any comparison,"
She said, "works for the Greek.
You hoard her, for art's advantage
But never for love's sake,
A perfect master coin
With which to test your mintage—

As if such test could prove
My virtue. Listen, if you,
Buying a cold kiss past,
Will let Troy's burning go,
Where's virtue? Shall I love
And she whore to the last?"

The Carpenter's Flute

*"All, however, that these thinkers [those Aristotle is challenging] do
is to describe the specific characteristics of the soul; they do not try
to determine anything about the body which is to contain it, as if it
were possible, as in the Pythagorean myths, that any soul could
be clothed by any body—an absurd view, for each body seems to
have a form and shape of its own. It is as absurd as to say that the art
of carpentry could embody itself in flutes; each art must use its tools,
each soul its body."*

—De Anima, *Bk. I, Ch. 3*

And if in the lucidities of heaven's
Cerebral blue the bloom of chaos spread?
Time slope and slop and slew the ark awry?

In the wigged years, that time speech glittered
Like the candles branching upon intaglio'd walls,
My hammer clanged those square-wrought nails home

In a house for pigs where I heard piggy speech,
Or once, a slave in Carthage, I planed beams
In the shipwright's broiling yard, and no doubt wept

My fortunes after hours, I don't remember.
The meaning is always now, and now is a florid
Monkey making dirty disorder in

Our tree; the which disturbance I had thought
Was opportunity for underlings,
The gift of music and a tone to tell

The blue that had been mine as much as theirs.
But all's at odds, wrong bodies and wrong souls.
I've read more books, I say, in these two decades

Than in twenty centuries, my head spins,
My mind whistles, and my arm aches; my hand
Must grip the pencil like a hammer claw.

Life is a job in someone else's shop,
Tools misplaced, the materials old and tawdry—
What can one do but do the best one can?

If it must be a tune then let it be a tune,
Broken and strange, this message from below.
Listen, for God's sake, to the carpenter's flute.

The Event Itself

A curious reticence afflicts my generation, faced with the
   holocaust;
We speak seldom of the event itself, but only of what will
   be lost;
We, having betrayed our fathers and all our silent grandfathers,
   cannot cry out for ourselves, the present and tempest-tossed.

But many things and all manner of things will be hurled
In a force like dawnlight breaking, and the billion bagpipes of
   our screams will be skirled
Stupendously month after month, the greatest pain ever known
   in the world.

There will be some instantly indistinguishable from the molten
   stone;
But most will have bleeding, burning, gangrene, the sticking-out
   bone;
Men, women, and little children will be made pregnant of the
   nipping crab whose seed will be universally sown.

In the screaming and wallowing one thought will make each
   eye stare,
And that thought will be the silence pressing down at the end
   of the air,
Soon to smother the last scream forever and everywhere.

For the last man in the world, dying, will not know that he is
   the last,
But many will think it, dying; will think that in all the vast
And vacant universe they are the final consciousness, going out,
   going out, going out, with nothing to know it has passed.

I Have Said Often

I have said often how one word
(As tongues of huge bronze bells will toss)
Can writhe and tumble in my head.
Listen: *loss, loss, loss.*

Never to walk down Franklin Street
In night's and autumn's trembling rain,
Two in the shoplights, bittersweet,
With gingerbread for a brain;

Never to watch December's eve
Design snow veiling in your hair

But just for a moment, and then turned his blank eyes
Into my face and went back to his chair.
And now I have written—certainly not a poem,
Only a marginal note
On the long book of the snow.

The Saving Way

When the little girl was told that the sun someday,
In a billion years or a trillion, will burn out dead,
She sobbed in a fierce and ancient way
And stamped and shook her head

Till the brown curls flew; and I wondered how,
Given the world, given her place and time,
She should ever come in her own right mind to know
That it all may happen one day before her prime,

The lights go out in one crude burst
Or slowly, winking across the cold,
The last and worst
That the old time's craziest prophet had foretold;

And I wondered also how she shall come to find
The town whose monuments
Are the rusty barbed wire rattling in the wind
And the shredding tents

And the street where the bodies crawl
Forever and ever, our broken dead
Who arise again, and again and always fall
For a word that someone said;

27

Or how she shall seek the plundered isles
Adrift on the smoking seas,
Or the desert bloodied for miles and miles,
Or the privacies

Of Jews laid out in a snowy woods,
Black men laid in the swamp,
All in their sorrowing attitudes
Of inquiry; or how when the wind is damp

She shall come someday to the marble square
Where papers blow and her father stands
In idle discourse with a millionaire
Who will rape her later on with his own hands;

And I wondered finally how all this
Will be anything to secure
What she knows now in her child's instinct is
The sole world, immensely precious and impure.

My dear, will you learn the saving way?
And then can we go,
In keen joy like Lear and like Cordelia gay,
To invent our lives from these great days of woe?

part two

Thou didst love the tiger, him of supreme necessity,
And then for him thou diggest seven and seven pits.
—*The Gilgamesh Epic*

The Light of Arcturus

Of irreproachable intellect is my lady.
   She dearly loves, not me, but the famous te
Of philosophers whose page burns bright and
   As Arcturus burning there across the ni h
   She does not care for my so ignorant vi

Mind, says my lady, is this transcending order,
   All-of-reality absolute and secure.
And what shall I do in love but try the harder
   While Arcturus gleams, a gem across the
   To seek my lady behind her veil of cold?

She speaks as if in dream she were dispelling
   Some curious evil. In flute-cold tones she tells
Of Bishop Berkeley and Kant, of Hegel and Schelling,
   And Arcturus shines like ice across the night;
   I listen, wondering what she truly says.

She points to the star to mark its place in the pattern
   Of infinite consciousness clean and bright and vast,
But to me the sky leers down like a dubious slattern
   And Arcturus wallowing there across the night
   Is a drunken eye aflame in a bloated face.

Worse, this same light cast by the starry litter
   Decays on its journey through the reek of space
And enters my eye like a seepage of rancid butter;
   I peep at Arcturus far across the night
   Like Coelacanth peeping above the slime.

How could what came fortuitously and lately,
   This orphan sense in an overdeveloped nerve,
Compose reality solely and so sedately?
   Arcturus! Moving forever across the night,
   Laugh once, once only, tip us one wink of scorn.

I doubt if a rational universe had wanted
   A thing that knows and calls itself a self.
Ghosts are the least befriended by the haunted.
   Arcturus, wheeling high across the night,
   Your licking radiance fills my skull like sand.

My lady's world, and mine. Is mere opinion
   What makes her welcome where I seem outcast?
Which view is right, identity, disunion?
   Silent Arcturus sails across the night.
   Against my view reserves a task for love.

Burning Dawn

      This day lies under glass,
      A relic. Blear and wan,
      Two feet wade up the dawn,
      Tread and fall back like fish,
      Two fish as blind as bone.
      The sun, the sun beats down.
      A vitreous, brittle sky
      Expands to the breaking point
      Like burnt glass being blown,
      And the blind feet go on.
      Nothing can keep it now,
      This sky that splits apart,
      For the cygnet and the swan
      On striding wings have flown

Over the shallow hill,
Dripping across the lawn
Droplets of breaking laughter
Like that of the soulless girl
Who was here and has gone.

Another Burning Dawn

Morninglight fumes among the houses
Like cooked phlegm. Waking in summer
In America so often only arouses
A landscape where one has never been,
Green forests in an equatorial war,
The succumber and the conqueror.

A vegetable kingdom: tumid leaves
Of trees like discus-throwers pump
The atmosphere, virulent juices
Sluicing through an immense digester.
Blooms sing like rubies. The vines
Grow and crumple, arise and fester.

Not Jew, not Negro, not heir nor scion
Of a dying house, and no more mad
Than anyone, the waker lifts an eyelid
Like a stabbed arras. *Libertad!*

In the garden in a humid haze
A zinnia with arms like anthems
Wrestles and humps, scourging itself
For the greater fury of these days.

Imaginary Cities

1. MONTPELIER, THE WINOOSKI RIVER

Streetlamp, river, bridge, snow falling,
Flakes settling, snowflakes lolling
On the brink of dark. The streetlamp, an exudation
Ancient and yellow, always receding, always
Decaying. Quickly, quickly eyes follow
Figures of the complex snow-crystals
That flutter, that skim and wallow
On the light's philosophical bleeding
And then drop past the brink, plunge
To the black water. Time after time expunge
In winter's ruined cone of night
These morsels of light,
Receiver and giver.
O river, river, river, river, river.

2. NEW ORLEANS

I am a trombone. By the chinaberry tree,
Under virgin's bower in the purple air,
I made a dirty noise you could almost see.
Arabesques edged the house with care
And voices crumbled in a distant square.
O King of the Zulus, consecrate me!
Mamselle's gown was a laugh of lace,
Band played "Dixie" at a thumping pace,
Moon sprawled low with a fire in her face,
And I brayed just once, deliciously.
Man said, "Boy, don't you know your place?"
O King of the Zulus, consecrate me!

3. Salt Lake City

When the great golden eagle of the West
Circles this capitol's dome, his wingtips
Ring on the mountains' bell
And the fountains of the sky drench us
In gold. Imagine every white stone,
Each citron brick, immaculate as cloisonné.

                                 The eagle,
Turning outward, perceives the salt desert
And the bleached skeletons reposing there,
But our streets are straight as our hearts
And prosperous as faith. This is the place
We call the great golden city of the West.

Like the rattler upon the mountain, we
Are free, aloof, but when we strike we warn.
We say we have made the dream of the West
Come true, and the centuries
Pivot upon our clean hearts which know
Success in America, death on the western
Trail, starvation singing through marimba
Ribs, the salt desert, and crazy religion.

4. Venice

Goldwork from the sea, blond yet bearing
Intrinsic shadow, darkness, a green
Of parts, aquamarine, all true seafaring
Countenances, incrustation, filigree
Worn to a fluid thinness, the long-striding
Arches. Still, beaten gold of the sea,
Tresses of the girl lazily breasting
The tides of the square. Late dusk, odors
Of wine, musk, hues of vermouth in sea air
Deeply enfathoming all open spaces.
The impassiveness of mermaids' faces,

Shell-colored skies, an evening breeze
Like a small exploring current underseas.

5. LENINGRAD

Wind sits in the Finland quarter,
Shrieking. The pale palaces,
Hunch-shouldered, lean to the gale.
Clam-colored Neva is frozen, an alley
Of molybdenum. A broken-winged news-
Paper flaps on the ice in ministerial
Desperation.
              A city is a million
Eyes, squinting in the wind.
And the poor half-blind palaces—
Even their old façades are bruised
In the wind's thump, thump, thump.
Indoors a fungoid rime grows
Up the curtains, ballrooms retain
No tinkle of minuets, nor mirrors
Any sparkle of rockets that once
Sky-plumed above the canal.
Overhead a gull trudges against
The wind.
            St. Petersburg!

6. CHRISTCHURCH

That city was colored by Marsden
Hartley. Gulls and windlasses
Cry at Port Lyttelton
On the same note—buy, sell,
Sell, buy. Slate-blue skies, full
Of lambs' wool, drop off short
In the South, the mansard
Of the world. Why
Have streets been made narrow
In a modern city? Processions
Of houses, white doors, a brass

Plate for every address. Fate
Has made this place to be not poor,
Every man is an alderman,
Teacups and keys
Are important, peace
Is important, and worship
Is important.

7. LÉOPOLDVILLE (c. 1959)
A shadow hangs down a wall like a curtain.
Ring,
    ling,
        somewhere a telephone confuses
The silence reposing in white and black.
At the sign of the egret the milliner snoozes,
Puffing his cheeks in the heat, certain
His half-dressed seamstress is safe asleep in back.

Anent Socrates, or Somebody

Old friend, it's easy. However you behave
The end's the same, you may as well be brave.
I wonder though, can good form now make up
For when you called me Sophist? Ah, the cup . . .

Abelard at St. Denis
(The philosopher contemplates his recent misfortunes)

1. NIGHT
Calamity's done. One seeks a rigorous brevity
Of mind, hard lest submission's posture
Should leave all haplessness only a fool's sport.

But I grow soft; now flesh like soft alabaster
Undoes the sharpness carved by spirit's severity.

I heal, soreness unknits, the rub of fattening
Thighs grows familiar. After all, I'm forty.
But Lord, youth did rush out in a sucking hurt!
Monked. And love is the loss, the disparity,
The gain. All's told. Hurt is all understanding.

What I know now I know is no way treason;
The gain inversely fills the widening loss;
The part thus cropped becomes the saving part;
Sex stays in wisdom like the thrill in grace;
Flesh spends itself for love of God in reason.

2. MORNING

Well, the mind keeps going. This morning
Brother Buttery discovered a mouse in the churn—
Round and round, frantic, scattering dung.
A mind? A world. Anyway, things keep going.
At six o'clock—there!—the sunlight brims
Like wine on the eastern hills. Sky's glazed urn
Tilts and drenches us with the Orient glow
That sparkles, and then floods, in our vague valley.
The shadows lunge and fidget, ewes of fear,
And where the larches preen their night-damp wings
A fox, I think, departs in humorous thrift.
The weasel cuddles home his purse of blood.
Far in the woods the songlarks plead for their lives.
And then what more lies eastward, past the hills
Falling to Indy, murderous, serene?
Our molten sun rills flashing down the rim . . .

That way lay God, upon a time in Asia
When cedars, feathered white in starshine, stirred
With night's extreme alarms, and constellations
Of very old and very sad desires

Drew to the mind grave rectitudes of heaven;
Then came rouged dawn with fervor-hued belief.
I wonder, could their mornings darken this?
Regard, shamed heart, the princeps walks. But splendor
Fails! Fails me and fails this valley. Cold gold
Of vacant radiance suffocates the stars
Like fish in a poisoned pond and makes our moon
No more than a dried onion hung on a rafter.
The planet tips on scared perspectives wailing
Across the void in crescendos for no ear.
Reality is a vast and drafty barn.
Manure and broken straw, dead stars in the mow,
The dust settling; and a hurt flea skulks behind
His piece of filth in safety. But what spirit
Inhabits here? The high east window breaks
In a gash of light like Cyclops bleeding. All
Upheaves, spinning, sinking, a qualming yaw,
Time-blinded, spun through the soundless arcs
Of freezing, a glass man flung to eternity
In one splintering moment of stopped frenzy.
Falling, falling; down the East forever.
O God, retrieve me, catch me in your arms,
My heart's gone dead with fear.

                              So instinct cries,
The little high voice in us always wanting
A god of larks and roses, the head
Gardener. My voice pipes too, a boy's
Again. Those Levantines, in their enmyrrhed
And balsam forest, history's predecessors,
They saw God in them as a children's god,
Rightfully so, and wrote him down for us.
But history grows, we cogitate its end
Viciously; not change, not the widening
View. And as accretions of experience
Divaricate our memories and build
The many-sided man, so God assumes

Intricate proportions, such as we know
In stained-glass dawns, a thousand lights assorted
In one richness. Fear too conforms, my stuck
And squishing heart lugged in my tumbrel ribs—
A piece of God. And so each spore of knowledge
Our consciousness entices from the world
With all self's rubbing wiles, each image
Transmuted through unnumberable resemblances,
Burgeons as self's grown substance, and is
Our sight of God, our vision. He cannot grow,
Surely; but vision grows, the self acquires
In each felt image brought to consciousness
Another inch of God, another touch.
And so—perhaps a garden after all.
Reality is an orchard all in bloom.
I love the self that is an apple tree
Whose ontologic bloom each season mounts
In panoplies of astonishment from the juice
Of root-strivings. I love roots, the members
That fork and search, acceding not one shred
Of inviolability to any fragment
Of the dense incorporate world. Vision grows.
Beyond the vision each man's ignorance lies.
Luck may uncover it in a blinding gift,
But hearsay never. Well, praise to the gifted.
But praise too for that lowlier way, a life.
The stern cognition and strict imagining
In which experience builds the complex soul
Of God, wherefore we hoist this germ (lost, lost!)
In relay down the course of time: a life.
At last the day leads my eye to a valley
Whose beauty still resembles dawn and dark
Beneath the larches, thick in the rowan trees,
Close to the chapel spire.

                    The day begins.
The scuttling rudiments of light take form,

Calling the mind to light. One thinks of all
Its shapes and figures, how it fills the mind
With almost every texture of memory.
I think of light that drifted on a beach;
Say moonlight, say a beach in Brittany,
The moonlight torn by furious clouds, the beach
Strewn with the huge black awkward rocks that clamber
Like crippled horses out of the sea; a wreck
Somewhere on the farthest rocks, and on the beach
A windy point of brightness, a fire. The flames
Call testily to my eyes, brandishing faces
Salt-stung with survival, those I hope I love.
The moon, staring obsessed and calm behind
Wild hair, withdraws my gaze steadfastly, showing,
Beyond the rocks in gray phantasmal light,
The marshaling misty legions that sweep on,
Forever on, murmuring the damp hymns
Of the null and indecisive wind. The light
Alone creates these images, and flows
In infinite similitudes among them,
Fusing the bits of meaning, brilliant silks
From which the tapestry of person grows,
Fluttering like Byzantium in mythic
Beauties, drenched in sense. The light: major
Or minor, moon or beachfire; sourced in the labyrinth
Of self's time-eating puzzle, whence erupt
By mirrored indirections our deep beams
Of instinct's savage delicacies of force,
Or that small angry fire of reason. Something
Like this, the light, figures our agency,
Our image-welding consciousness, our being,
Intact as structured time, compounded knowledge;
And yet no agency will move alone.
The fuel here is affections. Our motive is
Our love, love being the ground from which all other
Affections rise by differentiation.
If newborn infants tried to say "I am,"

Could it be anything except "I love"?
Feeling, like the heat of fire, combusts,
In first necessity, the actual spark
Or node of consciousness, yes, *is* that spark
Constantly burning and escaping, spread
In resonant ego's—

        Lord, I'm out of breath!
What was it you desired when you created
The philosophical temperament? Not this,
I dare say; stumbling, tumbling, bumbling;
Words piled up like jackstraws, and as steady.
All to say, "Look, look at the boy there, look!—
Stepped from the scullery door to fling his crumbs
To the doves." At once all curves, brow, knee, buttock,
Flow, flowing in light—*your* light. Brilliant!
And this is what I know, since I am for once
Absolutely honest. Oh, yes, that gemmed blaze
At the back of the void, that excruciating light—
Someday perhaps, someday. I am this product,
Abelard, a fire kindled from many small sticks,
And my light burns, though wanly, still with warmth.
Light to light, light in light, light for light.
I divide, Lord, like the fireflies, taking from all
And scattering again to all. And dare I,
Lord, therefore praise her—

        that one, the woman,
Beauty as prime experience, breaking?

        Praise
Her hair, flowing; saying of its softnesses
How candlelights were sieved to find them, saying
Its odor clung in thought like old forenoons
Of Spanish oranges lain in the sun, and saying
Its color spilled like cedar hearts split out
At some woodcutter's clearing; yes, so flowing,

Spilling, consuming every sense, and I
Only a burning face upon her knees.
Her hands were principles of song. Her mouth
In smiling moved like blossoming intricacies
On an apple bough, in sadness lay like a killed
Finch, in love was candy. Her voice was a plum.
Her body was so prompt, so grave, Lord, so tempered
(As for lute-playing), so erudite in half-dreamt
Secrecies, so genial in every coign
And crown of touchliness, so featly true—
Philosophies in each soft inch of her!—
That I despised my own, the ill-done brute,
Jagged, obscene. Yet put him to good work,
Such as he favored; and later memorized
Nine freckles. Above all, praise her eyes: eyes now
Of jasper, now of jade, of chrysoprase,
Emerald, viridian, all greens of lakes
Of Ireland, seas of Persia, of Alp moss,
Danish lichens, eyes of the fields of Flanders,
Of August's storm clouds leaping, blackish leopards,
Over the Seineside, eyes of the rowan leaf
Fragile as twilight, and swift eyes of wings
Of dragonflies, eyes of the bronze patine,
Of shards asparkling where the wine flask fell,
Verdant eyes, hazel, émail, red-green
And every greenery, green eyes I've roamed
In tropics glad with many a mystic beast
Of joy, dark with shadowy beasts of doubt,
Green eyes made parables of greenest texts
As dawn undid our fervors with the stars'.
Alas! Was so much cherishing in vain?
And is that luster falling from the world?

Where's brevity now? In my lady's eye?
We keep time strictly here. The refectory glass
Is Fat Jacques' duty, turned each night at compline.
Is it the sand, running, that whips our thought

To symmetries, reductions, causal dreams?
The grains drift down like Héloise in tears.
I mourn the cone below, the cone above.
Brief mind, don't let your crumbling tempt brief thought!
If only each grain were a painter's view,
Gold leaf and blue enamel, laid precisely
In individual strokes, innumerable
To prove each hour's exact complexities—
Then time would serve! Damn all simplicities.
Numerosity counts, the whole seethe and fettle.
Damn, damn all brevities!

                    The day begins.
The gaunt sun climbs. Let me take and cherish
Every impression. See, our goosegirl goes forth,
Such brave littleness shrugging her long dark hair
On a corporal's shoulders, scolding the pawky geese
For goosely sins, rubbing her eyes in sleep.
Our loves are flowers she wears without a thought.
And what girl with nine geese and April blowing
Will come this dusk with snowflakes in her hair?
Ah, I have seen the green bird come to sit
In a golden tree whose leaves are beaten gold.
It sits, and then it flies away again.
I am a—well, a sentimentalist
With something lacking (God!), and hence am driven
In guilt's awful contraries to submit
Desire to its opposing reason. Let
This be my desperation, as it is.
I can see no cleaner way for man's despairs.
So Héloise—a most egregious nun—
Is my thought-nutriment; no watery maxim
Served on a page, but so expressly felt
And proximate in my remembering skin
It stands me like a meal; not, certainly,
My sister clad in a kite (what hurt and beauty
Linger there is another part of wisdom),

But all I own and am, my selves, my beings.
I lose them, they slip away, the person
Stands gaped and shredded like a poor comical ghost
Caught in a cannonade. Yet a remainder lives
And the brilliances infold, each small part
Marries the others in a dense increase
Like a chapel window greatly inspirited.
The soul augmented from one scantling glimpse
Of somethingness caught here upon the glass
Pierces the gradual cognizance of God.
The green bird sits within the tree of gold.
Dear Lord, I love you. I, no man, no man,
Castrato squeaking from the guilty knife,
Flesh of no gender, tumor swelling here,
Alien, a shame, a shortcoming, tub of fat.
And I groan with love. Lord, was it that gay knife,
Dancing on me like the finger of last desire,
That struck the fear of man into my heart?
Fear is a saving, most instructive love.
I thank you on my rotting knees this morning
For all our wounds, each stroke done and received,
Without which not one man could heal again.

A Pseudo-Prayer

Again the November skies and their black wind
In depredation purge the maples
Whose brown leaves, flowing, rattle through the mind
Like tides on a stony beach. Sky's opals,
The watery sun and the mist-enmantled moon,
Revolving, lead the days around
In obscure succession, and the ground
Hardens where I tread cumbrously and alone.

No sound is more man's thought when he is alone
Than these dead leaves in their wind-seething,
Fretting and scratching the wall all afternoon
Like harsh decrepit winter breathing.
My cheeks are parchment. Then what holds me here
When the house has so much warmth within,
Except cold longing for my kin
Nearer to me than any at this door?

My child would be a stranger at my door
If there were a door where I was master.
Door and daughter, two-thirds of man's desire,
Fled in the wilder third's disaster,
And I am the stranger now, begging my keep,
Pacing a strange dead garden alone;
This northern wind won't touch her town
Where she forgets me, even in her sleep.

And yet she came once. While she lay asleep
I watched. I think no other vision
Of helplessness can make me want to creep
So much to prayer, though my contrition,
For all its grave validity, leaves me still
A man who cannot pray. To whom
Must I speak then? To Chance? To Time?
Hear how I wish her wise and beautiful.

It would be strange if she were beautiful,
Bearing my stamp. Strange if that fashion
Were hers which gave to Ovid's world a soul
In heraldic formalities of passion
And even now will drive a schoolboy forth:
Splendors our Shylock still defiles
In love purveyed with toothpaste smiles
And beauty audited for its money-worth.

But let her have such beauty as is worth
The hard work of the heart to purchase,

Her intellectual heart picking the dearth
Of thought's teeming, scanning the urges
Of pain's shrewd unities. Let her have this:
A face love-conscious of the bone,
A body cunning in skeleton
That, giving, keeps what no man may call his.

And let her lover know how much is his.
Let him, possessing, still relinquish,
And in good grace, that part whose synthesis
Of wordless claims can still distinguish,
As he cannot, her shimmering, tenuous,
Multiform, and radical self,
Her wholeness saved in his behalf.
So he shall have much beauty in his house.

I wish her too an old familiar house
Whose rites, inherited and formal,
Will shape love-faring. But *pouf*, that wish-mouse
Goes scurrying! Lack-form is normal
Now, rootlessness and fatherlessness
And houselessness. Let her not forget
The heart as source of form then. Let
Her ceremony be her own noblesse.

My wish is just this wisdom, this noblesse.
What is it but the world's election
In her knowledge? Reality's access
Will come, will be, in her perfection
Of knowing, but quietly. Opinion dwells
In half-awareness, faint, abstract,
But the whole woman lives in fact.
And she will cherish this as nothing else.

Finally may she find, beyond all else,
Some useful image of a father.
I don't know where or how. The daylight falls

Now, shattering quickly like quicksilver
Fled among the maples. May she find
Forgiveness for that poem I wrote
About the son I had not got.
The doorway beckons; this is a bitter wind.

Études de Plusieurs Paysages de l'Âme

1.
After the fire came rain.
The burnt-out forest
Hissed quietly; its ash
Foamed in cottony mire.

Sky flowed like protoplasm,
Thinly. The silver face
Of Edgar Poe declined
In the dogeared West.

We were all very dismal.
But smiled when a baked pig
Danced through the charred twigs
With a blue cup in its mouth.

2.
The storm came Monday night. On Wednesday we
Took wreaths to the point and flung them in the sea.

The sun shone, and the waves—oh, how they sparkled!
Even the gulls' shrillness seemed sweet that day.

Sweet too the piquancy upon the breeze
Of stranded whale, burnt oil, and ambergris.

3.

On a page of the unabridged dictionary
An H was lost. He had come willingly, had bought
His own ticket, his own costume, but now
The Annual Masked Ball of the Société
Des Logogriffons seemed too much for him.
Was no one to blame for his shyness and awkward
Manners? Every room, halls and stairways,
The alcoves and the mysterious cells above,
All were crowded with masked figures, graybeards
Of China, lascars, priestesses, troubadours,
Karl Marx, the brilliant Juan, Achilles,
Orpheus in at least thirteen incarnations,
Guinevere and Iseult, the lascivious girls
Of Dublin and Odessa, Tehran and Seville,
Who were, it seemed, as likely as not young men.
And such perfumes!—snuffed candles and wine,
Hot draughts from below bearing fierce bouquets
Of liquor and incense. Laughter flared and fell,
Provocations and delights behind the curtained
Recesses. The lost letter wept secretly,
His desires drenched his heart, and the band played
There'll Always Be an England all night long.

4.

Will not the summit offer views
Of all our homelands spread below?
No, no, the fighting winds confuse
Each vision in exploding snow.

I knew a girl who dug a hole
In my poor skull and took my soul.

Only the winds contest this star
Whose death we note with some surprise.
I wonder why we climbed so far
To plant the flag of paradise.

She put a spud in there instead,
A hundred eyes now haunt my head.

5.
Olive trees wrought from crude bronze. The sagged sky
Pebbly and rank, old
Lemon rind. A raped voice abrades the end of day.

Small animals, perhaps lizards and mice, the color
Of clotted blood, play
Dead. Do they move when no one's looking?

Some distance away the sea with great regularity
Clangs the land like a cracked
Gong. In the grass a vermilion plume, leaking.

The voice chafes in time with the sea: "Tell this
To Alcibiades,
We'll raze all Greece before we yield an inch . . ."

6.
I strolled the waves from Tampa to St. Pete
While flying fishes swarmed beneath my feet
Like green grasshoppers. Bits of antic foam
Were daisies nodding in the fields of home.
The sky's impearled loudspeaker arched the bay
And Lester Young boomed changes all the day.

7.
At dawn the desert turns to porcelain.
Upon a dune-rim stands a skeletal horse,
Head down, forehoof cocked, cropping glazed sand.

The stars blanch like goldfish in a frozen pond.
A lizard darts from the F-hole of a violin
That lies in perfect syntax on the sand.

49

Sunrays set the horse on fire. Behind
A giant cactus a shy Indian screams
Century after century in his death pains.

Billie Holliday
(1915–1959)

Here lies a lady. Day was her double pain,
Pride and compassion equally gone wrong.
At night she sang, "Do you conceive my song?"
And answered in her torn voice, "Don't explain."

Algeria

Years gone by in Chicago once
The Chalk Man came on an April day's pastel,
And ever since
My business has gone ill.

Because one day as I came home from school
A trilling woman spilled from an untuned house,
Thrusting her child
Into my arms; it jiggled, looking droll,
But she was wild
And ran beside me like a wounded horse.

The doctor said what could be said;
The thing I had been carrying was dead.

It was heavy;
Resilient, rubbery, collapsible;
Unbalanced inside like a bowl of gravy
Or a water-filled rubber ball.

That was an image of death.
And my waxen father orated in his casket.
And during the war
The crashed bombers had people underneath,
Though they really were not people any more.
We fished them out and put them in a basket.

Now I am thinking of the lovely land
Where palm trees more beautiful than herons
Sleep and stand
One-legged by the waters, and the flowers
Caress the old men in their barrens,
Pouring out splendors upon forgotten powers.

They also have bodies there,
And blood on the paving stones,
A bad smell in the mountain air,
Dead bodies, dead bodies, old meat and bones.

And the white-capped seas grope down the coast,
Pale hands beseeching, cold and lost—
So many. Yet the sea is blue
And all that red has vanished long ago.

For God's sake, stop, please stop.
Isn't this good faith
In your bodies' breath
All you can hope?

In Memoriam
G.V.C. *1888–1960*

These words are written for the Christmas season,
The first that we have spent without you here.
  And though you, unbelieving, taught

Your family your own way of thought,
Still this year is our richest, poorest year,
This Christmastime is ripe with spirit's reason.

Our richest and our poorest year—yes, both.
Poorest because it was the year you went,
    Taking your wisdom, kindness, touch.
    True, we weren't loving overmuch,
And yet we grew in your love, quietly spent
And now all spent. Such loss dissolves such growth.

The richest year, too. Your success endures
And must endure, must heighten in your going,
    Because now we define again
    Your hope, your serious faith in men
To save themselves. In this we will keep growing.
For this our Christmas and this poem are yours.

Trinidad

"Things are hopeless here, you know. But outside of that, man, life isn't bad at all."
            —*The remark of a native, quoted in* The New Yorker.

Yes, dear myselving isle,
It's winter here and I do age and ail;
On one creased haunch
The old bull bleakly leans in trampled corn
While snowstorm's ash
Fills up my North America like an urn.

But your rum-colored eye
Amid disheveling seas keeps frost at bay
With moony winks;

Although perhaps you need me, island mite,
All your green kings
Having absconded to the superstate.

A hopeless match, I know,
Though once I longed in secret and afar.
Now drumbeat cold
Bruises a mind born puny, drubs my words;
Someone more wild
With genius for your warmth is what you want.

Think. Is not need cheap?
And cheapness not most dear to lack of hope?
If youngsters tend
The supersystems let an old man praise
With eyes half-blind
Your fronded locks and wide blonde beachen thighs.

So we may take account
Of our unfitness. You shall win a note
Of fame perhaps,
And I—well, when the systems lose me here
I'll look you up
In my green atlas. You at least are there.

I'll slink dream-fashion past
The jealous seas that cobalt round your coast,
And our long loss,
So much, so many schemes, so many lives,
Will make us wise
To one another's guilt. And so to love.

It is cold. Dead cold.
The staked-out cub creeps whimpering round the pole.
Upon my ribs
Crawls this same mantling freeze that dumb and blue
Winds down the globe.
Stiff skin like sod locks in the graves below.

Will it not reach you? No,
You still outlast me but at last you'll die.
The munching surf
Someday, someday will crop your merest blade
And all the brave
And particolor joy cry to the void.

This is the hopelessness
Behind the others. Old men plant their kiss,
A yes upon
This book, a bronze or stone, the simple ground,
The warming sun;
Eternity's antiphon is no, is no.

Grandeurs to come and past
Must misconstrue me in their terrible waste.
Shun that mistake
And I will husband you like my good fire
Of salvaged sticks
The while my lungs sip this bone-picking air.

We work—we must—apart.
It's possible, your life against my art.
Call it caprice,
But at the last I'd have my deep blood spurt,
My bone sink piece by piece,
My precious purses spill into your heart.

Ontological Episode of the Asylum

The boobyhatch's bars, the guards, the nurses,
The illimitable locks and keys are all arranged
To thwart the hand that continually rehearses
Its ending stroke and raise a barricade

He left that house in the dirty day
  And no one said good-bye,
And no one knows where he went to live,
  No one but you and I.

Sometimes My Huge Death Rips

Sometimes my huge death rips me not as rude
As these unweaving others that will be.
It seems so strange. The burden is, for me,
An hourly argued bargain to conclude
With breath and burning in ingratitude,
And yet my anger loves them. Two or three
Who die in fate therefore are in me free,
While I shall go down merely unsubdued.
And these, sometimes when I hook back my fear
From that whirlpool the sucking pulse sets up
In dropping fissures of the lonely breath,
Come gravely, touch my arm, speak in my ear,
Tell me their names, bend to the spaniel pup,
And say good-bye, and go away to death.

Thalassa

In passion I bent to the march, treading, treading,
Comrade to all but most to obedient women,
Yet hung on their last resistance, so degrading
A treadmill, hung on the speck of the superhuman
In passion's depths denying my urgent reading
As if it were an impenetrable omen
In the bowels of love, or as if I were parading
Falsely among them, the pimpliest catechumen,

Until my sickness came and I lay still.
Abandoned then in that country for a long, long time,
One day I heard in my head like a distant bell
The sound *Thalassa!* And as the hawk will climb
In an empty sky, look down, and plunge at will,
I saw to their naked hearts, the foul, the sublime.

Alive

I used to imagine we were a fine two-headed
  Animal, unison's two-tongued praise
Of fastened sex. But no, though singly bedded
  We went separately always.

When you burned your finger and mine smarted
  We had neither one body nor one soul,
But two in bright free being, consorted
  To play the romance of the whole.

It was good, else I had surely perished.
  In change may a changeless part survive?
As it is, crippled in the sex I cherished,
  I am full of love, and alive!

Analogy Between a Certain Lady and a Field Mouse

Both are small and agile and active, brown
Of countenance, so simply soft that hands
Move toward them without thought. Both love
The country and do not love the town,
Except by dread fascination that betrays them.

If in a cold year one comes in your house—
Field mouse or lady—do not hunt up your trap,
For little harm is done by a wild thing;
Their pillaging is all a kiss or a candle
And they are gone again when it is spring.

Finger Painting on an IBM

Into the rhetorically celestial harmonies
Of your eyes, as a feather falls from nowhere
(Trailing nowhereness like a veil of waltzes)
Into the zinnia garden, I fall, my dear.

Among the flowering constellations there
I weep and sigh, and then I laugh and sigh,
Already forgetting to remember my vacant home,
The purged attic of philosophical despair.

Forgetting my errand too. What was it?
Did I bring you love? How could I bring
What I did not possess? How could I give you
Something thieved from me long, long ago?

It is possible to speak of a feather falling,
It is possible to be Shelley on an August day.
So much is possible that is not profitable.
The feather floats down to entice the child's

Tousle-fingered admiration. One thinks instead
Of ashes collapsing—a burned book, for instance.
So many fragments of what once was, so many,
Drifting in your eyes, my dust blinding you.

Not a pretty figure, of course. It makes my eyes
Smart terribly just to write it down. Yet see,
Settling and diffusing, they run away
Like ripples lightfooting across a pool,

And the constellations clear, the zinnia petals
Burn distinctly again, and the faller vanishes.
I am conscious of moving far underneath, a note
Winding like a hunter's horn through your blood.

Dark, dark. I did not know I could see in the dark.
And I have only to realize myself as my own desire
To have you sway and whirl in your dark spontaneity
Of dancing that you do not and cannot invent.

What power! I pulse in satisfaction. Something
From nowhere has turned into nothing somewhere,
Here in the fluvia of love, beneath the petals,
Beneath the stars, primum mobile, the cause of you.

part three

What! Have you come in the night?
Through the forest? Then you care nothing for tigers?
—*The Bhagavata Purana*

Poem

Autumn scuttles across these hills,
Cold wind and the ragged rain,
Beating, beating my windowsills,
Cold wind and the ragged rain,
But soon I am to marry.

Then that girl and I won't mind,
Hot in our January,
A time that beats or a time that chills,
Cold wind and the ragged rain.

Now

The fallen sun embraces
Tobey Woods,
Dark hemlocks and spruces,
All the dark gods.

An end of day. How many
Pitied the life
I showed them, yet not any
The harder proof.

Being is like a jewel
Warm with light
Whose origin and renewal
Is a cold heart.

But she, supernumerary
Of the last war,
Gone to the woods to marry
A philosopher,

She weeps. And so does Tobey—
My folk sorrowstruck.
The sun sets like a ruby,
Burning and dark.

Essay on Marriage

Snow came to us in the week of Thanksgiving.
I was studying Dr. Williams on the "variable foot"
  And Hölderlin on the necessity
    For writing one more poem,

And my wife and I had been married twenty-two days.
Not long, but considering the nature of
  Joy it was long enough. Because
    We each had known

Many bitternesses and disloyalties, and so
Recognized the advantage that loving brought to us
  After the ugly hope of solitude.
    We were very successful.

I was content to die. And when we went walking
We discovered many images of death: the gaunt and
  Skeletonized forest spreading its arms
    To gather cold flowers

From the sky, a pine seedling four inches tall
Mortified by a few ounces of frozen crystals,
    The trail vanishing among arcades
        Of snow-laden branches

Into the vague, expressive curtains of snow. Death
Was so deeply interpenetrated by purity and beauty
    That we clung together, whispering
        In awe, though no one

Could have heard us if we had shouted out
Love, love, love at the tops of our voices.
    By the time we returned to our cottage
        Rose Marie was crying

Inconsolably, for love, joy, the twenty-second day,
And perhaps, though she did not say so, for death . . .
    Measure, symmetry, these were ours. Yes,
        In each eye-turning

Down the forest's snowy avenues, and yet—
Has there ever been an invariable foot?
    Here I had wished a nude oak-torso
        Fallen the other way,

And there the brookside to break more amiably.
Even Rose Marie, who is a good-looking woman
    By any standard and almost unbearably
        Beautiful by mine,

Nevertheless pouts and looks away because one breast
Is a quarter inch more marvelous than the other.
    And why should I write one more poem?
        Will it save the world?

Will it save Rose Marie? I expect to write
Hundreds, but no great good will come of them.

Poetry, poetry, how many proud will die
   In thy service!

Poems will come inevitably like the seasons,
Imperfect and beautiful like the deathly woods,
   Expense of labor and expense of time,
     Like seasons and woods,

Like mechanisms, parts of a universe which means
Nothing, I guess, but simply moves, on and on,
   Imperfect and beautiful as only things
     May be that have no minds.

The meaning is all in my Rose Marie's tears.
We are grateful for their evanescence, creating
   Her the infinite wife, perfect and true,
     And me the infinite husband.

Christmas Package from East Germany

     The censor's stamp is rightly sullen,
     But the twig of the tannenbaum,
     The incautious candle, and the stollen
     Bring to a new bridegroom
     Something out of a world mad-fallen
     Possibly meaning home.

     Curious, this is a foreign odor,
     Yet I seem to understand
     The tanne as if it had spiced forever
     An old woods of my land,
     But O my father and O my mother
     How falls the censor's hand?

Godhulivela

The poets of the Land of Indra write
Godhulivela, end of day, "the hour
The cows make dusty," and a lotus flower
In my eyes lays its petals to the light

Of August evenings. Simply, this is how
The word in darkness lain two thousand years
And experience lost for thirty, hemispheres
Falling each way divisive of the two—

As we say, worlds apart—at last may join,
Something won back from chaos though by chance,
Godhulivela. The muddy cows advance,
Flicking their tails, Sad Udder, Bony Loin,

And Rolling Eye following one by one
Around the knoll, the duckpond, past the stile,
My lumbering, lowing, suffering, lingering file.
The saffron dust of evening cloaks the sun.

The poets of the Land of Tophet know
The word, could write it if they were inclined
To call that fading resonance to mind;
Their children would not understand them though.

The poets of the Land of Indra may
Consider this a mute and frightening end,
Something far too remote to comprehend,
But doubtless it will come to them someday.

Light in the Locust Tree

"My father was Menelaos, that homely king."—St. Agisthos of Samis

Light in the locust tree
Blown white, men say,
Was that lovelock; that eye
Was break of day;
Troy stares eternally
For those breasts' sway.

And maybe her mind was clean,
And maybe her sport,
But somebody was obscene,
Some crazy heart
Made beauty more than a man
And invented art.

She called the black bright ships
Dreaming to berth
Through all time's loom and lapse,
And then henceforth
A lie on a blind man's lips
Was woman's worth.

Ekstase, Alptraum, Schlaf in einem Nest von Flammen

Do not lecture me, doctor, about your science.
I sleep at night by a calm strong woman
Who dreams with her eyes deep-lidded in compliance
And with smiles, doctor, that appallingly illumine

Her sobs and contorted throat and thigh.
Doctor, her dreams are girl-breasts crushed to a rafter,
The rough wood, the held cry,
A rifle butt on the door, and drunken laughter.

It happens, doctor, I am tired to death of your skill
Because I have given and given and have no more
To give in the cause of such a smile
For a crazed Slav hammering on a farmhouse door.

Spring Notes from Robin Hill

1.
200,000 rhododendron blossoms I estimate
By multiplying the number seen
Through one pane of the "colonial" windowglass.
And I had wanted to show Rose Marie
A hummingbird, a most un-Silesian
Apparition: so she assures me.
Certainly one will come soon, I said.
Now the petals are almost gone,
Blown away like thoughts not written down,
And no hummingbird has visited us.
Probably they are becoming extinct.

2.
The birches in front of the cottage
Bow like lissom queens at the emperor's court.
To whom?
To me naturally.

3.
My German is awful, nine words mispronounced.
But a splendid language for bellowing.

When I find Tanio snoozing in a coil
Among my manuscripts, "Herauf!"
I proclaim, striking the air with my
Finger, "Herein, mein Herr Schlaffener!"
Nothing whatever happens. Tanio opens
One eye. "Kätze, was für hast du
Eine Attituden so gestinken!"

4.
Two lesbians live on the far hill
And keep the most beautiful garden in town.
Hyacinth and lily-of-the-valley.

Brother Marcus, make something out of that.

5.
Once we went walking in Tobey Woods
Leaving three loaves to bake in the oven,
And when we returned later than we had planned
The smell reached us some distance away.
"Oh—oh—my breads!" Rose Marie wailed.
"Ruined!" She fluttered her arms like a
Fledgling and hopped for home, clumsy
With the potbelly of her seventh month.

Not ruined at all, just good and firm
On the bottom.

6.
Fierce storms this season. Tornado warnings
From the weather bureau, and a sure-enough tornado
At Waterbury; many wild storms in the hills.
One day lightning struck our weathervane,
Busted the cupola, scattered slates every
Whichway, split a rafter, blew out the radio,
Entered the plumbing, and knocked hell out of
The curb box, making a pretty fair geyser.

Scared? Not me, I'd just had too many strawberries.
Rose Marie says I must make an appointment
With the Rev. Hebard right away, to be
Baptized before anything more happens.
I'm not much on theology, but I bet
It's not that at all. It's those bombs
They keep exploding out there on the ocean.

7.
A night in June. A new moon. Really,
On occasion the harmonies of the soul
Are too much.
                    Rose Marie walks under
The birches, and like them bending
Curtsies three times to the crescent
In thanks for a good conception, asking
That our child be beautiful and welcome.
So her mother had done before her
In a snowfield by the gray Oder, so
Her centuries-old grandmother had done
In the brown night of the Wendish forest.

Well, if it worked then, why not now?

8.
I
    to be a child of history?
                                    I
Determined by that tale of
    dutiful bloodletting?

However, let me speak now quietly
    without declamation
                        for I see
A fearsome thing will happen
    to my people—

Some lying at Concord or Shiloh
    or in France
                        and some others
Having also caught the grave-fever
    like cadavers well pleased
    and eyelessly rejoicing
                        in death.

See how they grow talons and
    lynx-tufted ears
                        —my people
    red-lidded in the night!

But Rose Marie was born on a
    crook of the Oder contested by
    three nations for three centuries
And she has the gentleness of the
    wood thrush in the cedar tree
    and no bitterness
                        though they
    drove her with pointed guns
    on the keen snowcrust.

In this cottage my history is—
    and my nation.
Quietly, quietly
    but with resolution
I will have no other.

9.
Solomon's Seal and Adder's Tongue,
Five-leaves, Columbine, Whitlow-grass,
The misty *Maianthemum canadense*,
Indian Cucumber-root and Bluet,
Saxifrage, Foamflower, Sweet Cicely,
Trailing Arbutus, Fumitory,
Wakerobin and the lovely *Trillium*

Undulatum and the Lady's Slipper,
Marsh Marigold, Bloodroot, Jacob's Ladder,
Bitter Cress, Toothwort, small Coltsfoot,
The Wayfaring Tree and the Horse Gentian,
My gracious, delicate *Trientalis,*
Rose Marie's honest Partridgeberry—
And boo to you, Tom, Dick, and Harry.

The Smallish Son

A small voice is fretting my house in the night,
a small heart is there . . .
                      Listen,
I who have dwelt at the root of a scream forever,
I who have read my heart like a man with no hands
reading a book whose pages turn in the wind,
I say listen, listen, hear me
in our dreamless dark, my dear. I can teach you complaining.
My father, being wise, knowing the best rebellion is at forty,
told me to wait; but when he was sixty
he had nothing to say. Then do not wait.
Could I too not tell you much of a young man's folly?
But you will learn. When you play at strife-of-the-eyes
with existence, staring at the fluorescent moon to see
which of you will go under, please, please
be the first to smile. Do not harden yourself
though it means surrendering all, turning yourself out
to be known at the world's mercy. You will lose your name,
you will not know the curious shape of your coat,
even the words you breathe, spoken out so clearly,
will loosen and disperse forever, all given over
to the wind crying upon distant seas. Moment of horror:
the moonlight will name you, a profile among fallen flowers.
Yet you may survive, for many have done so. You need

only to close your eyes, beautiful feminine gesture;
and do not be afraid of the strange woman you find
lying in the chamber of your throat. When a silver bird
strikes at the shutters of your eyes with his wings
admit him, do not attempt to tame him, but as he swoops
in the tall glimmer of your intricate room
admire his freedom; and when a silver mouse
scurries twittering through the passageways of your blood
consider his beauty. So it will be: dark, a long vigil,
far among splendors of despair, this creation
in the closed eye. Everything will be true, pure,
your love most of all, and your flesh in the drunkenness
of becoming a dream. Lingering among the revenants
who still bear your name, touching and kissing,
dancing among their tatters of skin and splintered bones,
noticing the song of the tomb, how it soars in dream,
you in your sovereignty condescending to song,
permitting your myth—what awareness then, what ecstasies
in the shimmering dark pool, what marvels of the dark stair!
But now, please open your eyes again. Have we not said
down with all tyrants, even our own? Especially our own!
Open your eyes; they will glitter from long sleep
with the knowledge of the other side of the world.
Their light then will be of such a quiet intensity
that smiles and frowns will fall away like shadows
of wild birds flying over. No complicity, no acquiescence;
and yet a degree of affection remaining, as when one finds
an old bible in an old cupboard of an empty house.
So it is, so, freedom and beauty. Do not be modest,
wear the delicate beauty of those crippled at birth
who earn the grace of their maiming. Do not be afraid,
assume the freedom of those born in their captivity
who earn the purity of their being. All one and all many,
but remember, never the two alone, falsely dividing
in the mind's paralyzed divorce. This is our meaning
under our true rebellion, this is the dark where we
may venture without our dreams. In the dreamless dark

where I await you, the dark light of my eyes
may still be darkly burning when you come.
You must look and you must seek
for my eyes will answer but I think they will not summon.
And if you do not find them, turn away.

The President's Speech

Before supper we had seen three grazing deer
in the frost-burnt asters at the forest's edge;
we watched them from the kitchen window; then we ate
our good meat and bread like any husband and wife,
and listened to the President in the radio under
the kitchen shelf. The night moved the mountain.
The box rattled, the voice told our exact danger,
taking course among waves of world-destroying violence
like a small craft sailing infuriate seas. We had,
we two, gone driven far about on the world's misery,
much shaken, but had come at last in blind luck
to settle at this way station by the woods. We shivered
again tonight, but consumed our meal somewhat hungrily.
"God save the deer," Rose Marie said.

Indeed, sir,
now I am alone and I am obliged to ask,
can you say, please, can you tell us what this is
that is necessity held in our sad hands? Innocence
will save the deer, I think, and all things loved
by Rose Marie; the quail whistling on Canaan Mountain,
the fox in his laurel, the gentian rusting by the brook;
innocence will almost save Rose Marie. No, not, dear sir,
their bodies or their souls committed to black fire
and the carious wind, but their minds that are their own.
Come, sir, man to man, now at one in the morning

before we walk out to the blast, would not this salvation
which we cannot, being men, esteem, nevertheless
be something? More than the appointments of history?
For once to think their thoughts and ask no due
in all the world of thoughts and things, nor take dominion?

Freedom and Discipline

Saint Harmony, many
years I have stript

naked in your service
under the lash. Yes,

I believe the first
I heard (living, there

aloud in the hall) was
Sergei Rachmaninoff

set at the keys like a
great dwarf, a barrel

on three spindles,
megalocephalus, hands

with fourteen fingers,
ugly as Merlin, with whom

I was in love, a boy and
an old man; a boy nodding

and an old man sorrowing
under the bushfire of the

people's heart, until he
coolly knocked out the

Prelude in C♯ Minor. Second
was Coleman Hawkins

in about 1933 perhaps.
I, stript and bleeding,

leapt to the new touch,
up and over the diminished

in a full-voiced authority
of blue-gold blues. I

would do nothing, locked
in discipline, sworn to

freedom. The years shrieked
and smothered, like billboards

beside a road at night.
I learnt how Catlett

drove the beat without
harming it, how Young

sped between the notes,
how Monk reconstructed

a broken chord to make
my knuckles rattle, and much

from oblivion: Newton,
Fasola, Berrigan, my

inconsolable Papa Yancey.
Why I went to verse-making

is unknowable, this
grubbing art. Trying,

Harmony, to fix your beat
in things that have none

and want none—absurdity!
Let that be the answer

to any hope of statecraft.
As Yeats said, *Fal de rol.*

Freedom and discipline concur
only in ecstasy, all else

is shoveling out the muck.
Give me my old hot horn.

Michigan Water: A Few Riffs Before Dawn
(In memory of Richard Wright)

1.
This hour is best, darkening
in absences; loud lights quieten
in a room in a city in the West.

Hour of calm, hour of silences,
silence lingering between the beats;
hour of distances, hour of sadnesses.

Listen, the softly thinking drum
measures the silence in which the bass
murmurs to make the meaning come.

Tranquilly my fingers contemplate
the bone they are, the bone they meet—
these keys breathing among shadows.

Silence holds the sweetness in the tune.
But now who cares? Will our affection,
the great slow sound, tell anything?

Visionaries sauntering in the sound,
you ten well-drunken in dark and light,
sing well, define, dream down the land.

What in the hour, and what in the heart
of sadness, sings in the song's shadow?
Sweet silence, is it then Chicago?

2.
Define. So the drum commands,
so the bass entreats. Define.
Ten black men setting out to dine.

Food of heaven had they none,
food of hell was so damned sweet
they sought and sought, and they had none.

The rope, the knife, the stone, the gun,
the train, the door, the cave, the tree,
the sign, the shutter, the snow, the dead.

Impossible to see, impossible!—
in the lake a wheel turning,
in the water a flaming wheel turning.

Like drowned rats, sodden in the dawn,
back through the streets they bring him
in dead march, the watery one.

Dawn comes to the city as to a cellar,
always gray, seeping, always gray,
and we call it, naturally, Pain of Day.

At one rotten moment of the light
the room stops, neither day nor night,
the music falters, neither black nor white.

3.
My brother and I, without hope,
set forth upon the city, going
in a white cart drawn by a black goat.

The goat was singing as he must,
my brother and I were not so brave.
The sun hove, shaken in his lust.

We stopped now here, now there
at rusty doors to take upon us
Godspeed and the departing cheers.

They gave us gifts of huge sums
of money. One gave his old coat.
Another gave his old fat wife.

"Good-bye, good-bye." We went on.
We were hungry. Near the airport
in a field we killed and ate the goat.

Nothing whatever happened, except
my brother who had been weeping smiled
and I who had been smiling wept.

Hence, scorched in that field, we knew
we were successful. When we returned
indeed the people gave us angry faces.

4.
Listen, in night's last tender hour,
listen, the somewhat stronger beating—
Chicago, our only city, speaking.

Steel: Shall I not, my children,
grow ever brighter, stiffening
against you my abominable beauty?

Concrete: Ah, I crumble! Back
to earth, sterile, changed,
a hundred lives at every crack!

Glass: Thought you would build a
museum case to house you? True enough,
I'll gleam forever. Wait and see.

Chrome: Even I, in my tarnish,
will stay forever in my opposition
to you: I can never diminish.

Brick: Your fathers knew something of touch
and skill and excellence in shaping,
something of gratitude; but not much.

All: Wind, water, stars, and all things
hard and mindless are our company.
Make your music; the night was long.

5.
My Chicago, city of all
the world, strewn
humble-jumble on a wild lakeshore.

We had at one time a beast,
a gorilla, famous among men,
and we kept it at the Lincoln Park Zoo.

In the heart of the city we had a beast
famous among men for power,
natural beauty, pride, and malevolence.

Its eyes bloomed like unlucky flowers
in a rock-cleft face, nodding in the wind
of emptiness nowhere beyond the cage.

The beast died prematurely of a heart
attack; which is to say, of fear.
And it was mourned almost everywhere.

The sun will shine in my back door
some day. But Lord the beast is taken,
taken Lord, taken and taken away.

Listen, the lake waters are seeping
in a thousand conduits, creeping
under the pavement. Listen.

6.
In the cage no word is spoken,
no power of darkness
covers the eyes with forgetting.

In the cage no amnesty
waits in the government of the days,
no behoof, no behest.

In the cage no listener hears
these superb particular concussions
of blood, neither a brother nor a sister.

In the cage the moon is irrelevant,
the sun unintelligible,
and the constellations unrecognizable.

In the cage laughter is courage
and courage is laughter and laughter
is courage is laughter is—*the cage!*

In the cage knowledge is the cage
and the comfort of knowledge
is an exceedingly narrow comfort.

Days succeed and fail. What more?
Nothing, except the murmured "no"
after the clanging of the door.

7.
Gray dawn seeping through stone—
see, the room blenches. Let the beat
intensify. Between bone and bone

the little blood aches with rain
and the tones deepen. Music!
Given all to Saint Harmony, all,

the pain, the awareness of the pain.
That is all. Music is heard
in one heart, harmony's great chord

in one conscience only; and yet
there is this not explained reaching,
touching, extending, as if the pain

could gather each of us to its own
being. Is it possible? The drum
murmurs against the graylight dawn,

the bass, in unison now, is calm,
the piano descends firmly. Chicago,
city of our music, the long "no,"

listen; the night was a good song;
and we are a true city, rising
in the unjust hour, honorable and strong.